# Unraveling Light

## Elayna Mae Darcy

Magic Key Media

*Unraveling Light*

Copyright © 2018 Elayna Mae Darcy.

All rights reserved. No part of this publication may be reproduced, distributed, or transmitted in any form or by any means, including photocopying, recording, or other electronic or mechanical methods, without the prior written permission of the publisher, except in the case of brief quotations embodied in critical reviews and certain other noncommercial uses permitted by copyright law.

ISBN: 978-1-73235400-5 (Paperback)
ISBN: 978-1-73235401-2 (eBook)

Book Design by Elayna Mae Darcy.
Illustrations by Elayna Mae Darcy.
Front Cover Image by Damian A. Falana.

Printing & Distribution by Ingram Spark.

First Edition, Sept 2018.

Magic Key Media
Philadelphia, PA 19144

*For my mother.
May we meet again
someday in the stars...*

> *"A book, too, can be a star, a living fire to lighten the darkness, leading out into the expanding universe."*
>
> **Madeleine L'Engle**

*I am unraveled.
A life illuminated.
Prepare to meet me...*

## *You*

First,
I had to collapse
and admit to the power
I'd given my name,
and know that it had
become a black hole,
consuming who
I wanted to be.

I came undone,
a revelation that lasted
twenty-four revolutions
around the sun.

Across time and space
who I could be
called out to me,
a quiet voice,
somewhere beyond,
out in the void.

Alone, in the silence
with fabric sheets and concrete
separating me from the sky,
I heard her.

I found her.

And though she
spoke in a whisper,
I knew she spoke truth.

*I am here.*
*I am light.*
*I am you...*

## *Lantern*

I illuminate the room.
By my light, your eyes can see.
Though I may burn out,
it will be to give you all of me.

## *Home*

When first I was here,
I did not know
my own name
or how long it would
take to become it.
I did not notice
the glorious willow trees
standing tall behind me,
for all I could do
was stare blankly
ahead to a future
filled with maybes.

Back then I was still
a newly minted orphan,
already feeling spent
after all the things
life stole from me.
But before me,
I saw an infinity of possibility.

I was sure, even then,
in the kind of way
one can't describe with words,
but can feel in the notes of a song.
This place was to become my Hogwarts.
It would always be my home.

And though this place is theirs now
so they might become and grow,
my heart will never leave here,
this I'll always know.

## *Named*

*That's not who you are,*
they said, as if
I don't know myself.
As if my heart beats
in their body,
or my thoughts sound
in their mind.

*It's hard to get used to,*
they said, as if
hurting me for their
own convenience was fair.

*Your name is X,*
she said, not
giving a damn that I
only answer to Y.

*I'm writing you up,*
she said, as if
by being cruel, she could
somehow also be righteous.

But those with hearts
spoke sweeter words.

*It's so you,*
they said, as if
discovering that this
was the missing piece
to my spirit's puzzle.

*It's beautiful,*
they said, as if
they knew how much
and for how long
my soul had ached
to be called that word.

*I'm so happy for you,*
they said, as if
their words were
the hands of a healer.

*This is me,*
I'd say, as if
it was who I'd always been,
because in truth,
it was who I always was.

## *Punctuated*

My body is an —,
some say it is unnecessary
or that it takes up too much space,
but it has a point to make,
and it won't let you go
until you've listened.

My mind is an !,
always running
high on energy,
feeding on excitement,
unrelenting and loud,
and ever without permission.

My heart is an *,
small, but important.
Blink and you'll miss it
but notice it and
you'll find clarity
and deeper meaning within.

My soul is an ... ,
Reminding you of more to come.
That the story continues
when this — body is done...

## *Starved*

Some nights I wonder
if anyone will ever
see me...
really me...
not the me that
embodies the body
that magazines
would have me be.
A monster by Shelley,
one that must be
trimmed, cut,
and spliced into
a societal ideal
of beauty.

No one has ever
seen me...
the real me...

They see what
the world has told them,
convinced them,
is ugly.

The size of my heart
amounts to little
when the size of my body
consumes what you
think of me.

You call me fat,
or heavyset,
not realizing you've
made my soul
the heaviest thing about me.

You've put me
under pressure that says
that the weight of my body
means I deserve
the weight of loneliness
on my spirit.

You've rendered me
beyond what a diet can fix,
because I'm starved
of love you're convinced
I'll never be served.

## *Life Sentence*

The depressive mind
has a problem with permanence
in which it convinces us
that every instance of pain
will be felt in perpetuity
for the rest of our days.
That one glance from a stranger
which lasted less than seconds is
a life sentence of
judgement and must mean
you are forever
ugly and unwanted.
The negative balance in your
bank account feels written into your skin,
forever inked so that
everyone sees and thinks
you will never amount to anything.

## *Atomic*

There are days
when getting up
out of bed
is climbing Everest
and days when
forgetting that one thing
you had to do
is an atomic bomb
in your chest.

There are moments
when just being in a room
with other people
is like 10,000 arrows
drawn and ready
to fire at your face
for breathing wrong.

When the world
makes you hate
who you are,
existing becomes
a wide open ocean,
and you don't
know how to swim.

## *Existence*

There's an ever
kindled fear that
this is it...
that I won't see tomorrow.

It's hard to shake
what's become fused
to my skin.

Will I still be
able to walk when
the shaking legs are
cut out from under me?

Will I still be
able to see when
my irises aren't
made of worry?

Will my voice still
sound when it has
screamed away
all its doubts?

Will I still exist when
I've stowed away
the worst of me?

## *Drowning*

I can't stop fearing that
I'll never get better
and that soon will come
the final storm I can't weather.
I'll drown in it
with no way out,
the waves so loud,
no one hears my shouts,
as water fills my lungs,
just like my doubts.
I'll sink to the bottom,
buried beneath the sea,
because I could never
learn to believe that
I deserved to be.

## *Will*

Typed it up and stared at it...
the little line blinking and
blinking and blinking,
a pulse
keeping with my own.

I want to press send,
but I think of who
my words might hurt
and I think of who
my actions might destroy
and I think of how different
the world will look
when I'm not in it...

Voices inside that
aren't mine whisper,
*just do it,*
*hit send*
*press delete*
*on your life*
*post it,*
*tell them*
*the world*
*how much you*
*think they hate you...*

Logic and reason
try to quiet the demons
that would have me believe
I'm worthless.

I must matter to
someone...
somewhere...
*maybe...*

I argue with the voices
trying to cast out their poison.

*I AM LOVED.*
*I AM WANTED.*
*I AM JOY,*
I scream at them.

*you are alone.*
*you are abandoned.*
*you are despair,*
they mumble back.

I erase the words
and type them again
and erase them again,
choking on air,
sobbing into my sweater,
as I read the words
one last time...

*If I died tonight, would anyone care?*

But my phone pings.
It's a snap from a friend.

When I reach to open it,
I see the brave kitten
on my home screen
as my hands are shaking.

But my friend wants to see me.
They want to see me tomorrow...

I glance to cards on a shelf,
sparkling with glitter,
and with love etched inside.

Beside them,
a pile of books.
Stories I haven't finished yet.

I'm sitting in a room,
with a roof over my head,
and a heater at my side
on a below frozen night.

I wipe the tears.
I erase the post.
I close the tab.
I reply to the message.
I feel something...

There's just an ember left in my heart,
but it's enough to spark a fire.

These times when loneliness
tries to take me, and when
the demon's whispers become thunder,
God whispers back, reminding me of my mission.

*Go on. Fight. Love.*

When I don't want to,
is when I must.
When I feel I can't live,
I will...

# *Sky*

Noticed a break of blue
in the cloudy, darkened sky.
A reminder that
hope and colors
lie ahead, if I manage
to stay alive...

## *Gifts*

Everything is a gift.

The reassuring ticking of a clock.
The quiet peace that ushers in winter.
The blanket tucked snug around my toes.
The starlight in their eyes when they smile.
The ink stains on my hands.
The hope I feel at dawn.

But life also gives us darker gifts.

The father who smelled like beer.
The blood in my eye from the rock thrown at my head.
The countless tears that stained my pages.
The bitter shiver of failure in my veins.
The mother who died in my arms.
The gnawing fear that I'll die
feeling the same way she felt.

...alone...

Every sadness,
and every kindness,
has been a gift.
Each one a tool—
palettes and easels,
brushes and paper,
charcoal and watercolors.
Every moment God gives me,
is another gift to help me
create myself.

## *Enough*

*No amount of you
will ever be enough,*
the voices say.

I've come of age
in a cold hard time
that has lied to me
so much and so well
that I'd grown to believe
they were right.

*You're not enough
because you weigh too much.
You're not enough
because you're broke too much.
You're not enough
because you love too much.
You're not enough
because you think too much.*

No matter which way
they cut me or divided me
or tried to summarize me,
I was never enough.

But I've had enough.

So I'll become more
than they thought I could
because I've always been more
than I thought I was
because the secret is
I am enough.

*enough...*
*enough...*
*enough...*
*enough...*
**ENOUGH...**

*The wind is howling.
The internet is screaming.
What a noisy world...*

## *First Memory*

It was an earthen rainbow,
a sprawling sea of leaves,
bright reds, brilliant yellows, fading greens.

My family's packed in the van.
Mom's driving, always steering
our family forward,
though getting no more
credit than a stranger driving a cab.

I know these things now,
for losing her taught me much
that I wish I'd never had to learn.
But I treasure those changing trees.

I don't remember the
90s song played on the radio,
but I remember that earthen rainbow.
I remember the September breeze
on my tiny cheeks
in the same way I
remember my mother...
with love, and with peace.

## *First Morning*

They made us wait
in the nice room
with the cozy chairs
and paintings on the walls,
as if the interior design
could calm away the chaos
of hearing the words
*I'm so sorry,*
*we did everything we could,*
*she didn't make it...*

Waiting for my sister
to arrive at the hospital
broke me only further.
I had always tried
to keep it together for her.
But this time I couldn't.
There was nothing
left of me to hold on to.

When we got home
from the hospital,
the rain was at last slowing down
and the sky became the
kind of golden rose that it does
after a fleeting yet powerful storm.

As I looked up to the heavens,
tears returned, and I raged that my mother
no longer stood on the Earth.
But I was grateful at least
that she had been welcomed home
to such a glorious, resplendent sky.

## *Your Name*

I wish I could have
known you before
a bottle became
your beating heart and
your veins became malt liquor.

I didn't know
until my twenties that
we shared a favorite song,
but by then it had been
ten years since you'd been gone.

I wonder often if you
could have been my friend.
If your heart hadn't
become a bottle,
maybe you wouldn't
have met an early end.

There's the dad I keep in my dreams,
who gave me books, cards with Snoopy,
and who sang me to sleep.
The memories with that dad are few,
but they're my most beloved just the same.

If only your blood hadn't
run cold like a beer,
maybe then,
I could have
kept your name.

## *They Were Stars*

My parents were always stars.
I looked up to them when I was small.
They glimmered bright,
giving me hope.
It was not until I grew up
that I learned they were
never as simple as
I believed them to be.

They were complex, flawed,
burning out, and farther away
than I could have ever imagined.

But even though
they have both long since faded
in their own unique supernovas,
when I look closely
in the darkness,
what light is left of them
still shines to meet my eyes.

## *Nostalgia*

The word evokes in most
Nickelodeon or N*Sync
or any of the other trappings
of our childhoods.
But for me, nostalgia has always
emerged in ways that
to the world might seem strange.

Backstage darkness,
the smell of lumber,
the hum of light fixtures.
12 scoop ice cream sundaes
from Friendly's after
every special occasion,
and lying in the freshly
mown grass of the football field.
Candle wax between my
fingers while lying on the driveway.
Nights looking for meteors,
and cool, rainy mornings
in the shadows of stone history
when we were hoping for a sunrise.

Nostalgia tastes like
Charlie's greasiest pizza,
smells like sweet incense,
feels like warm pavement,
and looks like starry skies.

## *Size of Stars*

I sit in the shadows
of these lording over towers
which reach up and up and up,
trying to shake the hand
of the heavens.

At night they become
citadels of steel,
with fireflies for windows,
illuminating the night
even as they blot out
the galaxies above.

Sometimes I wonder,
what are these towers
to the size of stars
or to the solar system?

What are these tiny
skyscraper toys to
the One who made everything?

What are fourteen stories of metal
to fourteen billion years
of stories that fill up the cosmos?

It is nothing shy of a miracle to
imagine that God cares
for these tiny skyscrapers
and the lives within them
as much as They care for me,
and for you,
and for all of the heavens.

## *Magic Hour*

Magic hour truly
is a name for a time
unlike any other.
What else but magic
could explain the way
the sun falls into
the bed of the horizon?
What else but magic
could describe the wonder
that I feel watching
silhouetted trees become
rogue brushstrokes against
a painted, glowing sky?
What else but magic
could express the promise
of adventure that lingers
in the air once stars
blanket the world?

## *Beacons*

Stormy skies.
Ideas about to pour.
Rattling metal cars
on rain-slicked rails.
But then,
OPEN YOUR EYES
AND I SEE THE SUNRISE.

Day's breaking as the night's falling.
Broken rooftops are racing by,
with fear bounding from
one to the next like a superhero,
chasing a masked villain they
cannot name, only to realize,
that the villain is all around them
and inside the walls.
The real villain is
the system hiding in the corner
behind broken glass
and used box springs
and the lie that
*you made this mess yourselves.*

The rain made everything greener,
but the sky's still getting grayer,
making murals into beacons,
the only reminders that life
and love and color
still exist.

## *Empty Chair*

The light is warm,
the feeling is comfort,
the aroma is robust espresso,
and the chatter is in
equilibrium with the soft indie music.

They all seem to be
functioning and focused and free...
though because I'm human,
I'm aware that's not true.

It's strange to explain
that I know we're all in pain
while all the while feeling
singular in my sadness,
and the thoughts banging
at my mind's door.

The souls you share space with
wouldn't notice if you weren't here.
The glint of amber sunlight
caught in your eye
would fall upon an empty chair
as if you were never there.

Even as the clownfish patterned pills
ease my mind, they don't erase
the latent pain or make
the sadness remain at bay.
But they keep me functioning, focused, and free
enough that I can try to be
just another face in the warm cafe light.

## *Every Corner*

Trading in SEPTA for the Sound
as a new adventure begins.
As I ride these new rails
through fog, my mind
becomes clear.

I'm meant to be here.

In this moment,
three thousand miles from home,
I'm by myself, but never alone,
because to every corner
of this world that I go,
God is with me,
inside of me,
and around me.
From Cecil B., to Othello, to Waverly,
the Spirit of all
that was, is, and will be,
is part of me.

## *Signs*

The sun sinks over my city.
Whiskey on my breath
lets me see her beauty
that's often hidden from me.
More sun stains my pages
as I write these words,
casting shadows of rings,
and fingers, and pens on
my journal's 6x9 paper world.

Through the window
there's a story made of signs,
and I can't help but wonder
what it has to say.

HERE YOU CAN.
ONE WAY.
ANY TIME.
ALL THE WAY.
STOP.

Brick after brick after brick.

EXCEPT PERMIT.
FOR SALE.
BEWARE.
DO NOT ENTER
THE GOSPEL.
ALL AMERICAN.
CLOSED.

A beautiful mural.

TRUE WORLD.
NORTH PHILADELPHIA.
THIS IS YOUR CITY.
NO STOPPING.

RESPECT.
WE MUST BE THE CHANGE.
EMERGENCY.
MAZES.
PAGES.
DIAMONDS.

Home.

## *Notifications*

The phone blinks and my heart jumps.
Another thumbs up for my existence.

The phone blinks and my spirit sinks.
Another troll drops in to say I'm #TheWorst.

The phone blinks and my mind thinks.
Another article that leaves me hopeless.

The phone blinks and my head shakes.
Another notification that I can't escape...

## *Shadows*

Figures pass me by.
Beyond the window they stroll.
Never touching me.

## **2018**

We didn't need Netflix
to end up in the Upside Down.
We built it ourselves
when we let truth
be burned to the ground...

## *Red, White, and Blood*

The saddest truth is
that we were never better,
and your "greatness"
was a myth and a lie.
Fed to the knowledge-hungry
minds of our children
so often and so young,
that before we even knew it,
we were addicts to the lie
of a free country.

We believed it was one
built on promise, togetherness,
and equality.

You branded it
onto our brains when
you forced us to stand
and pledge allegiance
to a flag made of blood.

Red blood,
for the lives lost.
The people you slaughtered
to build your picket fences.

Blue blood
is woven as the background to the stars,
because you believed your money
mattered more than lives.

White blood,
for your bigots who died
to "protect" a culture
that believed that those
who were black brown or anything other
deserved to be ripped from their mothers
to serve you.

As a child, I pledged to
your red, white, and blue blood,
not knowing the truth.
I thought the star spangled
colors stood for something good.

I wish I had known it was lies.

But when I look to the truth
with eyes wide open, I see...
This place was never free.

So I stand with the people
who don't look like me.
I try every day, to shut up
and listen to their truth,
their history— the honesty
classrooms kept from me.

I cannot change what's been done,
but I can help change what's to come,
with a mind that's open,
and with a heart beating as one

## *Believe*

There's times when
the way of the world
hurts so much that
I ask myself,
how did we get here?
How did we let hate
infect us when
our natural state is love?
Why are there so,
so many humans who believe
that fire and fury will make us great?

Vitriol bites with deadly venom
at the good and the light in the world.

Online,
in the streets,
in our hearts...
the poison seems to have won.

Yet the only reason that the demons
are so among us is because
we invited them in.
But they don't have to win.

A tweet, with love.
A smile on the street.
A hard conversation with a friend.
A willingness not to give up
even when all appears lost.
Hope can be eternal.
Love can be impenetrable.
Faith can be unstoppable.
But only when we believe together.

## *Still Beating*

When I look at all
the wrong happening
in the world,
I can feel my heart breaking.

But if I have a heart
that is breaking,
it means I have a heart
still beating,
and some days,
that is hope enough
to keep fighting...

*Magic in their smile.
Constellations in their eyes.
My heart's still. Waiting...*

## *One*

As a little girl
I dreamed in rainbows,
stars streaming through my hair,
chasing the promises on the horizon.

Fairy tales told me
one day my prince would come
and despite the princesses
that sometimes captured my heart,
I buried that piece of me
so well that even I
didn't believe it was real.

But then life got
RENT apart by a single word,
one that broke my world
like a sparkling geode cracked open...
bisexual.

A prince could come.
So too could a princess.
I was no longer a mermaid
without a voice.
I was no longer a sleeping princess
without a choice.

I was me.

Free to save myself.
Free to love myself,
to love anyone who
might become the one.

## *We're Here*

I thought coming out
would be triumph and kisses,
but too much of it has been
painful and dismissive.

Not gay enough to be gay,
not straight enough to be straight,
*You're greedy.*
*Confused.*
*Indecisive.*
*You're fake.*
I've become one of
the letters the intialism forgets.
To be bi, trans, or ace
means you're shown less respect.
Intersex, demi, pan, and queer,
we're tired of reminding
the rest of you we're here.
And so we fight for each other,
until equality is real,
and maybe then,
I pray then,
that our hearts might heal.

## *Stolen*

I asked you online before we met...
*please don't...*
Apparently you only heard
the first eight letters of my words.

I thought, *maybe I wasn't clear?*
*Maybe he didn't hear?*
I took on the blame,
and despite my fears,
I gave him the second chance
that all the "nice guys"
claim they are so deprived of.

But this time, I was firm.
*Do not kiss me again*
*until I tell you I am ready...*

He apologized, agreed,
and said he would respect me.

I wish he had left my mouth
as empty as he did his promises.

This time, unwelcome arms
wrapped around me, hands groping.
His lying tongue was down my throat,
leaving me choking on his words
that meant nothing, because my comfort
took the back seat to his desires.

He caught his bus,
leaving me on the sidewalk,
defeated, and full of a fire
that I wished I would never have to feel.

He never touched me again
because I never gave him
chance number three
to make a prop out of me.

But sometimes still,
I feel the smoldering rage
of the fire he started inside of me that night.

My first kisses should have been
decisions I got to make.
But ever since, I've fought to make sure
the rest are no one else's to take.

## *Loved*

It is hard to know
if I have ever been in love
when I have never been loved.

My remaining family does,
and so do my friends,
but when it comes to romance
it feels my heart may never mend.

I'm longing to know
if anyone will ever care,
but my hand keeps reaching out
catching nothing but air.

## *The Lesson*

I wonder what
we could have been
if you hadn't decided for me
that I was too good for you?
Maybe we could have been
if you had just believed
you could be cared about.

Though our time has passed,
I've never stopped hoping
that you found your happiness.
For even now,
I believe exactly what
I believed then...
you have always been
worthy of being loved.
I hope it is a lesson you have learned.

## *Read Me*

Sometimes I think in red ink,
constantly correcting my thoughts,
and crossing out the wrong pieces of me,
some days spent hating the lines
so much that I wish I could
rip out the pages of me.

I'm a first draft that
no one wanted to read,
a recklessly thrown together
work of prose left abandoned
in a bargain bin.

But when you look at me...
I become poetry.
I imagine if ever you kissed me,
we would become
a sweeping fantasy.
Your smile is my favorite story.

Yet the greatest tragedy
is that you've never read me.
What an epic we could be
if only I had the
heroine's courage to ask...
*could you ever love me?*

## *Our Star*

I watched you
loving her wishing ever
that I was her.

You created with me,
told stories with me,
and read into
the deepest parts of me,
never knowing that
I'd give everything
just to be seen by you
the way you look at me
in my dreams.

We captured moments,
we crossed universes,
we invented beings
and all the while,
with you never knowing
what you've always meant to me.

Maybe by writing it down
and setting it free,
I'll finally be able
to say aloud the unspoken truth.

Maybe you'll read this
and just know, or maybe all this
will fade at the end of this page.

But while I can't imagine
if you and me will ever
become an us,
no matter what,
there are remnants of my heart
that will always be yours.

In the corner of the cosmos
we created together,
a star will ever
shine for you.

## *Hiraeth*

Looking at your smile
conjures in me a hiraeth
that has nothing to do
with ground once stood upon
but everything to do
with missing the heavens
I am certain we were
sent to one another from...

## *Rebels*

To ask to hold your hand
would be an act of rebellion.
To kiss you
would start a revolution.
Maybe loving you
could save the world...

## *Waiting for You*

There's a perfect night
that we all wait for,
the kind that could only
be crafted in dreams.
In mine, there's no
dramatic carriage rides,
candlelit dinners,
or diamonds of any kind.
Whoever you may be,
it would be just you and me,
spending a summer night
on Rocky's steps while
it gets so late it becomes too early,
and together we watch
the sunrise over Philly.

We hold each other's hands
spending the whole night
laughing and talking and thinking
about the universe.
I never dreamed for
that mysterious one-night lover
that I would never see again.
I've dreamed of someone
so genuine and silly
who isn't afraid to be
hopelessly in love with their best friend.

I don't know if we've ever met,
or if you're still waiting out there for me.
But I have always known that somehow,
someway, this night I've dreamed for us
will come to be.

## *Harmony*

I worry that life won't
write me a love story,
and that my adventure
will be all on my own.

But then I remember
those who are with me,
loving friends, treasured family.
I'm never truly alone.

The stories made me believe
that I cannot live without them,
that my options are restricted
to a partner or to sadness.
It's taken far too long
for me to understand that that's madness.

I still dream of a love
that can last beyond eternity.
But until then I am here,
and until someone else
loves me, I'll sing
my own harmony.

## *Someday*

I tell myself it won't
always be like this
and that one day
someone will bind to me
like I'm their harbor
and my heart's where
they've cast down their anchor.

I've tried to imagine
who they will be,
but when your heart
can love his heart
or her heart
or their heart,
the beautiful possibilities
spin round in infinity.

Will she be a wonderer?
Will he be a dreamer?
Will they be a stargazer?
Will we become each other's?

Faith and belief that
the Lord knows my loneliness
gives me hope that
the space beside me
won't be ever empty.

But until I feel
their hand in mine
and until I hear
their name, it's time
for me to embrace my lonely
and learn to love myself.

*Words are in my blood.
My bones are built from stories.
Dreams ignite my soul...*

## *Torch*

I am leading the way,
journeying through generations.
I turn the darkness into day
so you might bring alive creations.

## Say Me

Gotta get these words out,
they've fermented long enough.
These vines of ideas
getting intertwined
in my mind until
a narrative pours.

Emotions demanding,
*Feel me.*
A story begging,
*Tell me.*
Words pleading,
*Say me.*

## *Correction*

They said,
*Your head is up in the clouds!*

I kindly corrected them.
*No, but my spirit is up in the stars...*

## *Creation*

There's nothing like
the pressure to create.
The way that a story
builds and blooms
in the mind feels like
a miracle every time.

Synapses are firing off
and then suddenly,
a hand is moving,
and ink is flowing,
until a soul is spilling over,
rushing and insistent
as a river set free.

Thought stained pages
carry the story.
Some days are beautiful,
bathed in glory.

Yet some still drip
with a depression so dark
and so deep and so dense
that it pulls me in.

Those hours, I become a star
collapsing inward, still breathing,
but scarred.

Though always,
onward.

Pain washes away
when joy surges forth,
and we are baptized in
the promise of tomorrow.

To create is to never stop.
It is to breathe
and to know
every moment
we grow,
and something new
begins.

## *Poetry*

Poetry is a form
of emotional osmosis.
It is absorbing the way
everything from the
breaking up of two people
to the
breaking down of North Philly buildings
makes you feel.
It is taking in particles
of meaning through your skin
until words begin
bleeding from the ink
between your fingers.

## *The Dream*

In my dream,
I knew the smell of time,
as I watched the birds
find home.

You kissed me
again and again,
as we ran the ruined halls
searching for something
we couldn't name,
finding nothing but
empty rooms and broken desks
and each other...

The tree tops
burned crimson as I sensed
the smell of time.
Then you kissed my neck
while all the birds found home.

## *Bloom*

The warm sun
on my back tries
to make doubt bloom
from my spine,
but with the words
and the meanings
and the questions
bound up in pretty papers
before me, I'm trying
to plant hope.

I have dreams blossoming
in my brain which
demons made of weeds
seek to choke out and kill.
But my still, small voice
reminds me to give
fear no quarter here.
When doubt screams,
love must shriek
and hope must hold
the fear like a friend
it once knew
who has changed.

The hope knows
that fear and doubt
were once flowers too,
but ones with poisoned soil.

So love and hope,
though small and quiet,
nurture and forgive
the fear and the doubt
until they remember their colors,
they remember their names...
they were once joy and faith...

Through love and hope,
they bloom once more,
and with the help of
the sun on my back,
the garden along my spine
blooms and grows and sings.

*Unraveling Light* • *Elayna Mae Darcy*

## *Power*

Universes in my fingers
bring words and worlds alive.
Star clusters in my brain
bring people and places together.
Infinity in my heart
gives life and love a voice.

God has given me
a sliver of Their legacy—
the ability to create.
They have given me
a nose to smell memories,
a mouth to whisper musings,
eyes to witness moments,
ears to experience music,
hands to excitedly make.
They have given me
all that I need for
a life lived magically.

Love and light,
imagination and dreams,
are more than sentiments,
they are our weapons.

I wield them knowing that
each moment that I fight,
and each moment that I create,
I am waging war on hate
with the sources of true power.

## *Rising Tide*

Don't keep me from dreaming,
plays the music in my ears,
as a mosaic of inspiration
settles and dries.
The people I've seen
and the dreams I've had
become one, because
like the Spirits said,
*a rising tide raises all ships.*

With their words
and their hearts,
new ideas flourish into being.
In this sea of creative minds,
I do not swim alone.
I am side by side,
swimming on together,
in a rising tide
that lifts us all.
You and me,
them, her, and him,
we and us.
We swim together
until we break the surface
and bask in the sunlight
of our dreams.

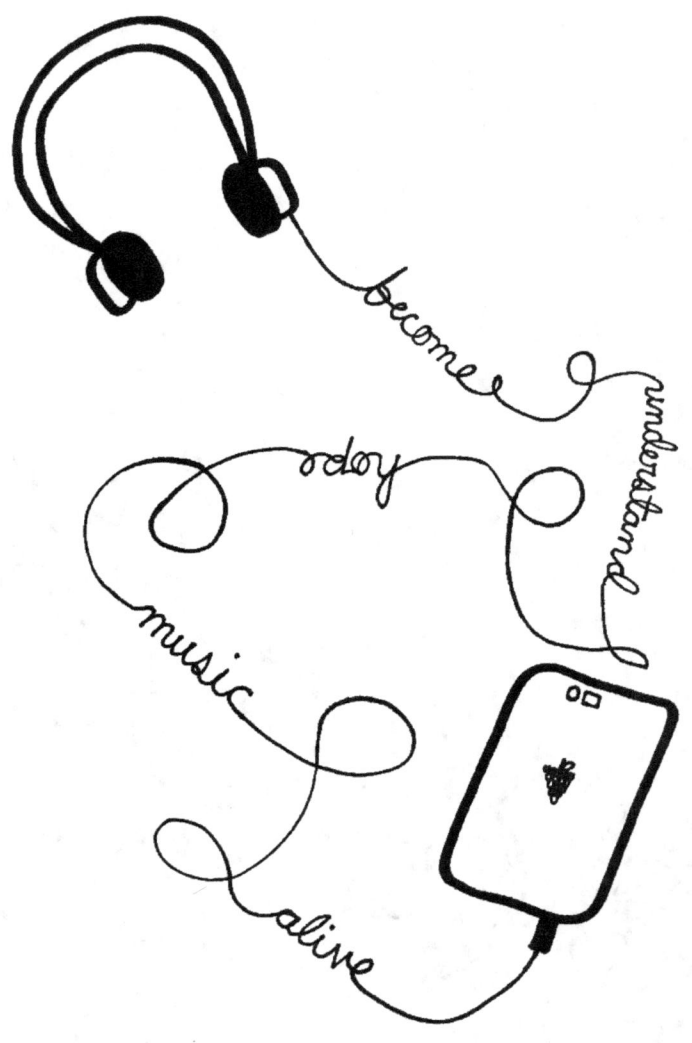

## *Inward*

With headphones on my ears,
the people around me become mimes,
moving their eyes and
mouths and hands,
saying things I can't understand
because I'm trying
to listen inward.

What does my heart tell me?

This I have always known...
I am meant to imagine and to make
and here among all this silent chatter,
I can hear inside.
Between the music
and between the lines,
hide words and hope
that only I am meant
to bring alive.

## *I'll Be*

I can only be
who I am for when
I try to be other,
it's a lie leaving me smothered
and crushed beneath
the weight of expectations.
When a pen is in my hand,
I feel my power surging,
my spirit growing into
the flower of the seed
it always was.
I don't rhyme all the time,
nor will I adhere to
the standards which steer
the ships of society's consciousness.
I'll be who the fuck
I wanna be because
all I can be is who
my maker made me.

Screw proper verse.
Damn the shoulds.
Destroy the demands
and fuck all the plans
that people think
they get to have for me.
I'll be the magic
that I imagine,
I'll be the dreams
that I fathom,
I'll be the strange
I hope to see in the world,
because I'm the only me in the universe...

## *Boundless*

I will never forget
    the moment I became boundless.
        There was a settling in my soul,
            a confirmation of truth
                in an instant...
                    I can create anything.

                      I'm home with
              a pen to command.
           I'm alive with
        a camera in hand.
      I'm breathing when
  painting things,
I'm believing when
    my voice sings.

        I am an artist
           who did not think
                outside the box,
                    but rather drew it
                into something new.
        I filled it with
      words and with colors
    and with all the others
I've ever made.

        I didn't let them
           tell me what kind
                of artist I could be.
                    I became the artist
                    I am.
                          Just me...

*inspire*

## *inspire*

i cannot know if these words will make sense but inspiration never really does it is this strange and ancient nagging in the deepest places of my being that begs me to be freed inspiration is leaping breaths and passionate fury leaving me teeming with magic bursting with wonder and longing to speak it is every time new and different and yet full of familiarity like a friend i have just met but feel as though i have always known it is butterflies beneath my feet lifting me towards the sun it is the smell that makes me time travel to places i had forgotten it is the way the wind on my cheeks when i close my eyes feels like whispered kisses from the cosmos inspiration has no form nor frame but is a picasso of abstract joy and chaotic pain that compels my spirit to create it is all at once a supernova of the soul an elegant ember of an idea and a cosmic complexity that has been waiting for me since cells formed and consciousness was born more rewarding than any achievements more fulfilling than any days labors more satisfying than sex inspiration feels more real than my body it feels more real than my fingers it is the same energy that i was forged from i am an idea made alive i am a spirit who will survive these words may not make sense but they are all i have to convey what inspiration has meant to me this child of the heavens who somehow continues to be...

## *Spirit*

Inside the skin of one,
I possess a spirit of many.
While I stand alone,
I'm made up of
millions of instances
of existences
of experiences
and of atoms.

I walk around with a body
that's lived on one lonely world.
But inside I fly free
with a spirit that's kissed
the edges of forever.

We are none of us one.
We are all of us many.
Plural singularities
made of matter
and memories.

*We break and we bend,
but we never stop being.
We are forever...*

## *Audacity*

Aspire to have
the audacity of the bud
that dares to bloom in winter.

## *Born*

Be who you were
before you were born
and you will become
who you were always meant to be...

## *I Am*

The sun comes out
but the ground remains
icy and cold and solid,
and it reminds me
too much of who
I can sometimes be...
a warm sun smiling,
giving what light I have
to the ones I love,
while inside and on the ground,
I'm broken, hardened,
and freezing to death.

It took an inviting,
an embracing of something
that made me bigger on the inside,
to understand that the sunny sky
could melt the cold below.

Because always and ever
I am both.
I am a world.

I am sunlight and snowfall.
Muggy evenings and bright mornings.
It is that always and ever
being everything all at once
that reminds me
I was never meant to be singular.
I am darkness.
I am light.
I am...

## *Highs and Lows*

Time ticks, unrelenting clicks,
a reminder of forward motion,
an insistent ocean with
a tide that abides by the moon.

I wish I could be as consistent.

For though I be persistent,
I can't keep my life
in time with a single rhythm,
a balanced ebb and flow is something
I have never known.

The world is ending, or all is well,
I'm basking in heaven, or drowning in hell.
Mastering balance ever evades me.
I'm a result of the highs and lows that made me.

I want to breathe even, to know calm and stillness,
but a mind ever on a precipice
is a penetrating illness.
So I breathe and use my pen,
to try and ease my mind,
so I do not succumb to
the highs and lows of time.

## *Keys*

My symbols of hope
left waiting for me
when I needed them most.

On the ground along
paths I hadn't walked before,
placed into my hand
when I needed to feel sure,
turning what I thought
were solid walls
into doors.

On the day I moved in,
and once when I moved on,
on the set of my thesis,
and my twenty-seventh year's dawn.
When I questioned my story,
when I was about to be hired,
they've become cosmic reminders
forged in heaven's fires.

Each key has a message
that I am never alone,
unlocking a way forward
to adventures unknown...

## *Beauty*

The Post-it on the mirror
spoke when I felt alone.
*You Are Art,*
the small paper said,
surrounded in hearts,
giving me reasons
to start to believe,
that this season of doubts
too shall pass.
It won't be long
until I'll be free,
joyful, and am finally
able to see my own beauty.

## *Sunsets*

Signals and sunsets and signs,
things that make us read
between the lines of our lives
to rationalize moments...
that which makes us alive.

To bear witness
to such things
is to know God,
to see creation,
and experience the sensation
of the souls we've been given
and know that the
universe is in our veins.

The power isn't just higher.
It's inside.
Always growing,
waiting with patience
for us to notice.

A priest's hands
or knees on a pew
are not what we need
to open our minds
or to know that love is stronger
and that hope lasts longer.

So until my final breath,
I'll keep a weather eye
on the horizon line for the
signals, and sunsets, and signs to remind,
we mustn't ever give in.
We must love, continue, and awaken.

# *North Star*

I am heaven's compass,
a guide from the dawn of time.
And though my light be ancient,
it has made wanderers into the wise.

## *Uncertainty*

Not long ago,
I befriended uncertainty,
taking what had once
been my enemy and instead,
choosing to love it dearly.
We talk often now,
late into the umber hours.
I ask questions to which
I have long wondered
what the answers might be.
Yet I am met every time
with a knowing smile
and an encouraging
whisper of,
*wait and see...*

## *Becoming*

Twilight and dawn,
are my beloved times
for the same reason
my heart belongs
to fall and spring.
Neither is complete,
they exist in flux,
always in between
in the process of becoming
something they weren't before,
but now will be until
a new day breaks.
I like to think
my spirit is a season
like fall or spring
and my heart is a time
like twilight or dawn.
For every fallen seed,
a new something grows,
and for every night
that the sun sinks into the sky,
in the morning, it always
and ever returns to rise.

## *We Are*

I don't know if I am any good at this but I know it is something I must do. If my brain isn't painting words or creating worlds it feels alone, haunted, and unheard. I dream to be seen as more than what I've been because when the world has attempted to interpret me they have always been wrong because all along they have eaten society's lies that to be a certain size means as a thinking, feeling being, you must be compromised.

This, I can no longer abide.

And so I keep writing with the hope that it will make society see I am inviting them into my heart to understand me and to view me more complexly as a being, who though maybe broke, is richly living life. I will not be bound by expectation, I will breathe in liberation knowing I am made as I am because my Maker has a plan for me to share my stories, and help others see their glory for we are all of us made of the same substance as the stars and the dust of the galaxies far, beyond what we've ever been allowed to believe that we are. We are warriors. We are wonders. We are scarred. But still, we are...

## *Coordinates*

An address only goes so far
in explaining where
and when we are,
for our coordinates
in the cosmos
matter more than
corner streets or
country crossroads
in the eyes of
the Artist that painted us here.

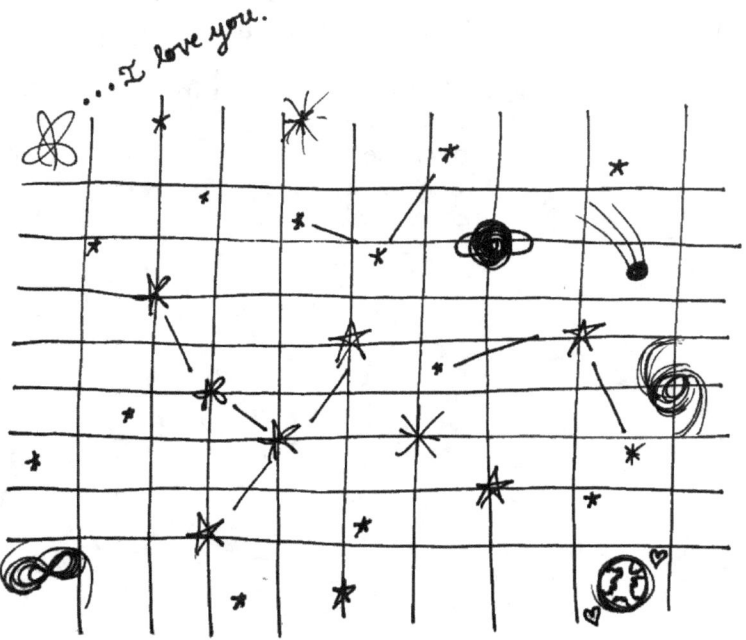

## *Storm*

Through thunder storms
And floods of self doubt,
I pull on my holey shoes
and keep going.

I don't know how,
but I imagine it is
thanks to my words
and my faith
that keeps flowing.

There's a current inside me
which I can't control,
an upstream rush
of stories and hope.

When I feel like I'm drowning
I'll remember to swim,
because I'm the
heart of a storm,
about to begin...

∞ ∞ ∞

## *Afterword*

The first printed (and digital) versions of this book were brought into existence thanks to the kindness of those who backed the book during its Kickstarter campaign that ran in April of 2018.

The days of that campaign were a whirlwind for me as a writer, and even as I finish readying this book for publication, I still find myself unable to believe that it is a reality now instead of just a dream.

One of the most special things about that campaign, was the event my friends helped me to host the night before it concluded. The event took place at the Warehouse on Watts in North Philadelphia, and it was the first time I ever read my work to an audience. The crowd was small. Only twelve people (including the friends of mine that helped me run the event) attended. But it was one of the most incredible nights of my life. We drank wine and talked about poetry and I managed to feel more alive than I had in a long time.

But of everything that happened that night, the most surreal moment was when after I had concluded the reading, one of the attendees who was a stranger to me, came up and thanked me for my words, and asked to hug me. They had recently lost their father and felt touched by my work. I was overcome with emotion. The next night, I wrote this final poem for them.

## *Brave*

You, brave child,
are the reason for my words.
The universe conspired to bless us both,
for in meeting and sharing our pain,
we can begin to recover.
Our shared hope, a healing rain.
They called me brave
for speaking my truth,
but the fact remains that
these words were
always for you.

# *Kickstarter Illuminators*

Thank you to the following magical individuals for being guiding lights in the production of this book by donating $35 or more to the original Kickstarter campaign. This book would not exist without your kindness and heart.

## Torches
Aaron Leighton
Ashley Craig
Chrissy Albeck
Courtney Stratton
Jessica Schlessinger
Katy Cartee Halie
Kristin Petroske
Laura Oleksy
Shannen Michaelsen
Sujin Headrick
Tal M. Klein

## Lighthouses
Alicia Bede
Alex Lowder
Patrick Annas

## North Stars
Damian Falana
Elan Samuel

## *Acknowledgements*

First, and absolutely foremost, thank you to my dear visionary friends. This particular project was born of inspiration bottled up from seeing all of you chase your dreams. It was through your encouragement and kindness that I was able to lock away imposter's syndrome long enough to finish this thing and share it with the world. To each and every one of you, my love knows no bounds.

Particular thanks are however required for several of you, for being my spine when I felt like I might collapse. Christine, for being my voice of reason whenever I was having doubts, and for always offering the kindest guidance in moments when I felt most lost. Cait, for supportively being the first person to fully read this thing, and always being a beacon of light in this dark, messed up world. Cara, for being a soul sister in crime, understander of all my feels, and believing in me from day one. I cannot wait for the world to know your name. And Elan, for being the best damn editor/human/friend/celestial being that I could have been fortunate enough to meet. You inspire me on multiple planes of existence.

To Catherine and Sophie, my dear magical friends. Y'all read the first few drafts, gave me invaluable feedback, edited this thing, and coached me through this process, giving me hope to keep at it at every turn. I love you both so much.

To Margot Atwell, the indelible Director of Publishing and Comics at Kickstarter, for taking a chance on me, and showing me so much kindness as I begin the journey of being a published author.

To Constance, for giving me that little poetry journal from Target for my 25th birthday, and sparking within me a love of poetry that I'd long kept buried. You have no idea the handprint you've left on my heart, even though we've still yet to meet IRL at the time of this first edition printing. I'm so glad we tumbl-ed into each other's lives.

To Damian, words will never ever be able to convey how much your support has meant me. Our vortexes, your encouragement, and your faith in me helped bring faith back into so many facets of my life. Thank you for being the very best alien I know.

And last, but very furthest from least, I have to thank my incredible sister, Sara, for getting me to read and write. You have from my earliest memories been there to instill in me the deepest, most miraculous passion for telling stories, be they blogs or poems or novels. There is no way I'd be who I am without you, your whimsy, your imagination, and your smiles, even when I know you were hurting. I don't tell you enough that I love you, so here it is in print 5ever. I love you, sis. Thank you for the words you've given me.

## *About the Author*

Elayna Mae Darcy is a professional fangirl, making a living by flinging her words and feels out into the universe. She's an annoyingly proud Philadelphian and Temple University alum, who spent her whole childhood dreaming she'd get to do all the cool shit she does in her adulthood. Her first short story, CONTINUUM, was published in the second issue of Wizards in Space literary magazine. She currently lives in her own imagination, which can be found somewhere between Hogwarts and a galaxy far, far away, and she is the proud mother of many plushies and fictional characters.

## *elaynamusings.com*

**twitter** | @elaynamae
**instagram** | @elaynamusings
**tumblr** | elaynamusings.tumblr.com
**facebook** | facebook.com/elaynamusings

. . .

www.ingramcontent.com/pod-product-compliance
Lightning Source LLC
Chambersburg PA
CBHW071212070526
44584CB00019B/3011